Dot-a-Saurus: Dino Fun with Dot Markers

by Happy Press Kids

Othnielia

Argentinosaurus

Spinosaurus

Euoplocephalus

Ankylosaurus

Nodosaurus

Apatosaurus

Quetzalcoatlus

Dilophosaurus

Allosaurus

Maiasaura

Velocisaurus

Protoceratops

Deinonychus

Pachycephalosaurus

Heterodontosaurus

Utahraptor

Plateosaurus

Cryolophosaurus

Diplodocus

Eoraptor

Tyrannosaurus

Parasaurolophus

Compsognathus

Velociraptor

Einiosaurus

Troodon

Oviraptor

Carnotaurus

Brachiosaurus

Edmontonia

Torosaurus

Microraptor

Brontosaurus

Stegosaurus

Coelophysis

Therizinosaurus

Kentrosaurus

Baryonyx

Triceratops

Citipati

Giganotosaurus

Suchomimus

Archaeopteryx

T-Rex

Stegoceras

Camarasaurus

Styracosaurus

Gallimimus

Iguanodon